Angels and Harvesters

Poetry by James Harpur

A VISION OF COMETS
THE MONK'S DREAM
ORACLE BONES
THE DARK AGE

Translation
FORTUNE'S PRISONER
The Poems of Boethius's Consolation of Philosophy

James Harpur

❧

Angels and Harvesters

To Betty,
with best wishes,
James

ANVIL PRESS POETRY

Published in 2012
by Anvil Press Poetry Ltd
Neptune House 70 Royal Hill London SE10 8RF
www.anvilpresspoetry.com

This book is published with financial assistance
from Arts Council England

Designed and set in Monotype Bembo by Anvil
Printed and bound in Great Britain
by Hobbs the Printers Ltd

ISBN 978 0 85646 447 8

To Evie and Gracie

ACKNOWLEDGEMENTS

Poems in this collection have previously been published or accepted for publication in the following: *Agenda*, *The Bow-Wow Shop*, *Cork Literary Review*, *The Guardian*, *Image*, *The Irish Times*, *Poetry Ireland Review*, *Poetry Review*, *Riddle Fence*, RTÉ *A Living Word* and *Sunday Miscellany*, *Shine On*, *The SHOp*, *Southword* and *Temenos Academy Review*.

'The Falcon Carol' was commissioned by Carol Ann Duffy for the *Guardian*'s supplement of Christmas Carols, December 2010.

'Finbarr and the Serpent of Gougane Barra' won first prize in the Manchester Cathedral poetry competition 2011.

I would like to thank Peter and Kit of Anvil Press for producing this book with their usual care and diligence, and Rosemary Canavan, Alyson Hallett, Mark Roper, Grace Wells and Ian Wild for their encouragement and wise insights, and also Mel and Pat, John F. and Mary, and Evie and Gracie.

I would also like to thank Pat Cotter of the Munster Literature Centre for all his generous support, as well as the Arts Council of Ireland / An Chomhairle Ealaíon, for literary bursaries in 2008 and 2010; and the Irish Funds of Monaco for a writing residency at the Princess Grace Irish Library, Monaco, in 2010.

Contents

Part One

Gougane Barra

'Tell me, then, and tell me truly, what land and
country is this? Who are its inhabitants? Am I on an
island, or is this the seaboard of some continent?'

Homer, *Odyssey*, Book 13, ll.232–35

Autumn

The leaves are falling, falling
As if from somewhere far away

As if from distant dying gardens in the heavens,
Falling, like tears or sighs released from darkness.

And in the night the heavy Earth falls away
From all the stars into loneliness.

All of us fall. This hand falls
And look at other people – it's in all of them.

And yet there's One who keeps this falling
From falling farther, endlessly, gently, in his hands.

'Herbst' by Rainer Maria Rilke

Reflections on a Baby Crow
in the Light of the Venerable Bede's Sparrow

I open up the stove to clear the grate
And flash! as if a coal has come to life
A crow flies out – I spring back with a shout
And watch it head towards the window glass,
Peck at the light in panic, try to leave
The wintry room. It flops beside a vase.
I scurry, open wide another window
Then run outside in time to witness
The nestling shoot out like a ragged arrow.

Later, I think of Bede's implicit prayer:
'We fall from glory to this life of darkness,
Blunder around mistaking glass for air;
Lord, help us find the straining hole of light
And leave for dead our temporary night.'

Osteopath

My back's a lump of clay, becomes a spine
Beneath your fingers, little hard-nosed creatures
That sniff out tangled nerves and sidelong pain
Autonomously probing with a blind man's
Feel for the beauty of a groove or contour,
Reminding me that I am skeleton.

Now on my back I see the skylight frame
A chasm of unboundedness, space blue.
A half-moon lit up like an x-ray
Tugs at my gravity. You're earthing me
With pressure: you rotate, push and pull,
Make new the muscles, tendons, of my body,
Create the definition that I lacked
So I may rise like Adam, ribs intact.

Dormitory

I   JUNIOR

For Peter Longshaw

The world is turning black beyond high windows.
We sit on our Crimean beds and talk
Guardedly, embarrassed by our new pyjamas;
Mr Macgregor comes and says a prayer,
We breathe 'amen'; he switches on the dark.
The clock chimes out the endless quarter hours.
Someone is tuned to Radio Caroline
And earplug-deaf intones a nasal chorus,
'I hear you knocking, but you can't come in';
Sniggers beget sniggers. A sleeper burbles.
I want to fall to somewhere else, like Alice.
Later, the moon pours in and makes things marble
And boys as peaceful as they were in wombs
Lie dreamless as dogs on medieval tombs.

II SENIOR

For Rob Jones

It's icy. I'm snug in bed. And Jones my mate
Is crouching down and whispering in my ear,
Suspiciously benign: 'James, you awake?
You'll never guess – I've got you out of Latin,
I've settled it with Neggers, you're in the clear' –
He knows how much I'm dying to believe him;
I dread that class, and now he's seized his chance:
'Relax, I'll run your bath and get hot towels . . .'
I close my eyes. I'm gone. And he's relentless:
'But first I'll bring the croissants, café au lait,
And then perhaps a fat, hand-rolled *Gauloise*?'
I dream of sky-blue France, of St. Tropez
And float in heaven . . . till I hear the bell
And Jonesy's chuckle fading into hell.

Gougane Barra

The mist sucks in our car to a world
That's pure except for leaves that drop
Like bits of flame or scraps of gold.
We arrive just as the drizzle stops;
The lake deepens the unpeeling hills.

The pilgrim hostel has no guests.
The chapel's closed; and at the well
We marvel at a sign's request
To refrain from throwing in our pence –
As if officials could outlaw
Whistling or smiling, song or dance.

We walk beside the lake, and sure
Enough the shallows buff a mine
Of coins, like amber eyes of fish,
That keep lit, and hard, the faith behind
The spinning moment of each wish.

Finbarr and the Serpent of Gougane Barra

Did it exist?
           For hours I'd scan the surface
Hope for a splash, a shadow in the water,
Anything
         to puncture the mysterious.

At night I'd set the traps with squeaking bait.
But nothing came
             except a badger and an otter.
Yet still I felt its presence by the lake.

At last, I snapped: I drove the serpent out
With curses, shouts – I exorcised the beast
Along with every slithering scaly thought.

But soon . . . I could not bear the certainty
Of absence, emptiness.
             I headed east
To settle where the plains of marshes lie

And built a trap, a cave-like oratory;
And here I pray for god
            to coil around me.

The Leper's Squint

(in St Mary's Church, Limerick)

A day the colour of old chewing gum
Darkens, then rain cracks and webs the Shannon
And drives me to the haven of St Mary's.
The grey Church-of-Ireland atmosphere
And waft of candles, dampish plaster,
Return me to an old ancestral past;
I warm to a heraldic wild boar
Who springs up on an oak misericord
And to the stillness, cool moist air,
White streaks of window light on piers,
Solidity of tombs, the stone floor,
Hymns posted like a cricket scoreboard.

But in the north wall there's the wide dark slit:
I imagine lepers lining up outside
Poking in fingers, like strange gastropods,
Impatient to receive the Lord's body.
For how long afterwards did priests recall
In dreams those hands, alerted by the bell,
Appearing as white vermin, disembodied
Tentacles closing round the bits of bread?
For how long did the visitants retain
The hope that bread transformed to Christ would shine
Inside their flesh, and heal, before hope died
Expelling them unchanged to death in life?

Outside, the sun is beating off the clouds.
Map raised, I guide myself from Englishtown
To Irishtown and cross the road to avoid

A bunch of ambling bristle-headed lads.
A tea-time drunk, his face as red as tongue,
Sways into me then stumbles on.
I feel embarrassed that others saw me flinch
And walk off mustering all my nonchalance,
Enter a café, mostly for a toilet,
Where everyone looks styled and confident,
Youths who cup the world in cappuccinos
And gaze beatifically at phones.
I find a corner table, disappear
Behind the curtain of a newspaper
And read the personal columns listlessly
Then daydream through my tourist memory:
The siege of Limerick, the Wild Geese,
The boycott of the 'Jewish colonists',
George Clancy shot by Black and Tans.

Outside, the rain is speeding up pedestrians;
I wait until it stops then gesture to a girl
Who finally comes over with the bill.
We swap pleasantries, but she talks too fast
As if to mask her Slavic gutturals.
I give a long-rehearsed spontaneous tip,
Rejoin the rulered streets of Limerick,
Weave in and out of groups of shoppers
Flowing and pausing, greeting one another,
Half-hope for little signs that I exist –
A tilt of head, a smile; but they walk past
Oblivious, as if I'm not quite visible
Or have a heartbeat like a warning bell.

On First Seeing the Book of Kells

I join the shuffling stop-start queue
As edgy as a mourner filing past
A waxy body in an open box,
I know I'll only have a minute
Or so, my eyes are two hair-triggers
I'm nearly there, nearly there,
Bang –
As if I've just been shoved on stage
Adjusting to the sepia audience –
I see the gospel squiggle into life
With oblongs, circles branded on
As frames to trap the golden bees
So quick they fly invisibly
But leave an afterglow in ribbons
Of countless plaited flights;
I'm looking at a dream
Cut out from someone's sleep and pressed
On vellum like a transfer;
Or a swathe of skin assaulted by
A mad tattooist, or a blueprint
Of creation by the Demiurge,
The planets spinning in his eyes
His paintbrush touching things to life
In ochre, green and orpiment,
Lamp-black and lapis lazuli;
Or a brain that's whirring inside out
Its ganglia revealed, lit up
In every synapse, curling fibre,
As by the electrics of a migraine
Or vision of Elijah's chariot.

Above it all St John looks down
A melancholy alchemist
In a lab of bubbling cylinders
Who yet again has failed to find
The lapis philosophorum.
The less I stare the more I see,
Letters begin to stir and creep –
Where is the Word? And what's this world
In which a peacock-headed 'n'
Resists the tendrils of a vine,
An 'i' pretends to be a harpist
Plucking an elongated 'c'
Or longship raised up on its end?
I raise my head to see the whole
And slightly blur my focus,
The letters seem to link together
There's someone nudging me to move,
Let it come, let it come,
Another thirty seconds, please,
And yes, it's there, pristine and freed
In
Prin-
ci-
pio erat
Verbum.

The Removal

In memory of Gerard 'Pete' O'Donovan

Incomers, we knew at once who'd be arriving
The way the door we left unlocked burst in
Like a police raid, or from a mighty gust,
The shush of boots and boiler suit divested.
Then round the kitchen door a film star's entrance:
Bright smile and bounce of sheep-grey curls, a glance
Towards his slurry-stained and steaming socks
Before he sat, leaned forward and relaxed.
So we'd conduct the mass of conversation,
The sacrament of tea with 'genuflections
Of the spout' to stir the leaves, and biscuits.
Although an illness lurked he seemed so fit,
Unfolding family trees, greyhounds, bowling,
Tugs of war, and who shot Michael Collins;
His high noon with a bull that stood its ground,
Bass growling, 'kicking up the sods', head down,
Until it backed away.
                              So gradually
We learned the lore of parish history,
Found bearings in new townlands, and new cousins
Among O'Sullivans, O'Donovans,
And bedded down our home; and had a daughter,
Who'll take her place among the whin and fuchsia,
And fairy forts, the river Argidheen,
Cape Clear and Galley Head, and standing stones.

                    ★

For months we missed the lights of his blue truck
Along our drive, the sheepdogs in the back;
Then heard he was a patient once again:
Trips to the Mercy, toxic medication.
And soon the dairy cattle had to go,
Perhaps a move of house; he didn't know.

★

That autumn night after his removal
He lay alone in limbo, his funeral
A dozen hours or more away; the church
Gathering emptiness around his box.
Asleep I heard loud knocking, so insistent
I knew it must be him, a revenant,
Perhaps with one more thing to say
Through dream before the burial next day;
But what his message was I did not know
Unless he did not want to be alone
In darkness, silence, cold, and so had swum
Towards our lights, towards the nearest home;
And still it came, that knocking, till I woke –
And flash-recalled the door and all we'd locked.

A Churchyard Ghost in West Cork

AFTER HORACE ODES 1.28

For Rosemary Canavan and Joe Creedon

Visitor, come over here and leave
The tomb of Smith, my fellow soldier;
His ghost has long since left his bones,
Which were discreetly bedded down
Like mine in corners of this graveyard,
Our little patch of grass and stones
Among the hills we loved, and feared.
We were, you see, two Englishmen
Buried among Cotters and O'Learys,
Neighbours in death, if not in life.
We may have lived a hundred years
Apart, but war remained the same
For both of us, the ambushes,
Assassinations and reprisals;
We did our duty to the death
And were disposed of in the bog
Which closed around our contours.
That Tartarean bog! It clings
To everyone without distinction,
The murderers and the murdered
The soldier and miscarried baby –
It's like a great enfolding memory
Spread out across this country's soul
Preserving all identities;
And it's a purgatory too
Leeching our blood and guilt and hate
To leave a husk of innocence.

Visitor, the bog returned young Smith –
He surfaced from the oozing turf
Within six months; the air still sickly
With burials and grieving for the dead
And sharpened by the bitter-lipped lament,
By the valley of Keimaneigh
I live where the deer come at night
For their rest . . .

                and Smith was laid
Within this ancient burial place.

And as for me, Lieutenant Guthrie,
All I recall are bullets faster
Than seconds, and the Crossley tenders
Ablaze and shouts and screams,
The pulse of running for my life,
Kneeling down among some trees,
And darkness filling up my head
The sense of flowing from my body
As it was sinking in the bog.
I stayed for half a dozen years
Before my body was exhumed
Reburied in this hallowed ground
Like Smith's. A heaviness, unease,
Remains in me: I can't remember
The killings, torchings carried out
And if I dragged my heels or not.
I pray that I was not the worst.
I spend my days in endless vigil
Watching the cars and tractors pass,
People scrutinizing headstones
And couples courting in the shadows.

Visitor, please, come over here –
Yes you who walk among the tombs
Towards the chapel, where you'll see
The only ornament is ivy
And windows frame the flight of birds.
Come here and say a prayer for me
Or place a flower on my grave –
Even a dandelion or vetch –
To help me leave this world. Do this
And you will have my gratitude
And blessings; please don't refuse,
Just think if you were in my place.
You may be young but days slip by
And *Omnis una manet nox*
There's one night waiting for us all.
I know you're in a rush, but stay;
It won't take long to say a prayer
Then you can go, rejoin your life.

Christmas Snow

Never came that year, and yet
It came in other ways, remembering the Light;
As suds frothing in the Garavogue
Around bridge arches, a scuttled trolley;

It fell from lamps in Henry Street
Illuminating tracer-lines of rain
And shoppers gripping rods of sleek umbrellas
As if playing giant straining fish;

It flickered as a candle in a window arch
In the round tower of Timahoe
But only some could see the eye of flame
Protecting sleepers in the graveyard.

It fell as stars above the Sugar Loaf
Lit up as cats' eyes by the gaze
Of a farmer standing by a gate
Above the mercury lanes of Wicklow.

And when the sun emerged from night
Snow came as seagulls spiralling up
Like bonfire ash behind a tractor chugging
Through slantwise fields near Baltimore.

It came as shoals of clouds held still
In the reflecting depths of Bantry Bay
And as three harbour swans
Turning their backs on the Atlantic;

And as sheets and pillowcases hung on lines
In Waterville and Elfin
By women biting clothes pegs, dreaming
Of visitors arriving from the east.

And it was found as ironed table-cloths
And icing knifed on marzipan
In kitchens dimming into evening
In Rossmore, Desert Serges and Kilbree.

It gleamed as circles of the host
For worshippers in churches lit at midnight
Amid cities ablaze like fairgrounds
Or villages as dark as silhouettes;

And it appeared in moon-insinuated waves
Unrolling across Long Strand
Rearing up like angels made of spray,
Roaring the word in tumbling syllables

Then sucking in their breath to whisper
It's Christmas, Christmas, Christmas . . .

Monte Cassino in Kerry

I see my parents standing there,
On honeymoon, in clifftop fields
Near Waterville the year beyond the war,
The summer so green it lengthens
Their nerves too long attuned
To the adrenalin of seconds;
The sky's a Mediterranean blue
Atlantic silverings beckon
Towards the Skelligs on the skyline,
The two of them before a life
That neither can, thank god, divine;
For now, they are at one, as man and wife.

My mother is painting a ruined house;
My father paints from memory
Preferring to the Kerry paradise
Infernal Italy;
His colours can only rise to shades
Of tree-bark or muddy brown,
Gun-barrel, stone and misty greys
To spread annihilation round
Cassino on a defoliated hill –
A monastery reduced to bones
A holy relic of itself, its walls
A line of fractured tombstones,
A graveyard in his mind
From which the dead pop out behind his eyes;
A weeping wound
No married love can cauterise.

★

Cassino came to shadow us
Above the fireplace in the dining room
Survivor of a world closed off,
The war a never-answered question
A mystery sometimes leaked –
My mother waking up to hear
My father talking in his sleep
His voice another man's, a soldier
Asking 'Where am I?', or just a shout.
My mother opening the back door
To sling the junk-shop German helmet out;
My father in the cinema
Shaking and sweating at the bomb blasts
On screen. The conflict,
Rolled tight within the past,
Kept trying to unravel, like the script
I found all spidery on his diary page
'No More Bloody War'
A madman's jitters, a child's rage,
And dated April '44.

★

Cassino shadowed him to London
And, post divorce, the flat he leased,
Resuming its role of skeleton
On the wall, a beggar at the feast.
It lurked among the marriage photos
Above the gold-stemmed lamp
The trinkets and mementoes
As seemly as a patch of damp;
During a dinner party's banter

It shrank from candlelight
A witness to itself, a sombre prayer,
A vigil through the night;
And when the sunrise hit the Thames
And lit the whole of Chelsea
It was content to wallow in its frame
Of mud-light, stumps of chewed-up trees.
How could a new wife share
That landscape and the frozen clues
To when the silent air
Would suddenly whistle lethal tunes.

*

After his death the painting stayed;
But when his widow died, the flat
Was cleared and it was borne away
By strangers to a shop of bric-à-brac.
And so the monastery
May live again through other eyes
On some new wall, now just a curio
Of history, anonymous,
Appreciated if at all for brushstrokes
Or composition and how
The tree stumps lead you up the slope
Towards the ruins on the brow;
A picture pure and simple; a fantasy
For children in a hall or kitchen,
A backdrop for make-believe,
A vampire's haunt, a lair for witches,
With all its imprinted death and grief
Relevant no longer.

And I hope if there's an afterlife
It will be similar with my father –
He'll watch his traumas drop away
As unemotive paintings of his past
Or rickety stage sets in a play
In which he happened to be cast.
And now perhaps he paints his life
The way it should have been,
His brushes dipped in oils of light
Creating scene by scene
New outcomes, his images
Redressing whatever they depict –
The sadnesses, injustices
And wounds received, inflicted.
Perhaps he paints a field in Kerry,
Includes himself absorbed in painting
The reconstructed monastery
All sunlit, and the olives shimmering,
A veteran walking in the foreground
Amazed to see Cassino now intact;
And draws my mother in that field
And shows the two of them enrapt
Communing with their canvasses,
With grass and sky, the briny air –
Receiving, letting go the pulse of happiness
That only love can bring; unaware
Of war, and of the fate which split
Them from the path they took together
That day of fields and sea-light –
He paints them painting there,
As if they had forever.

Part Two

Angels and Harvesters

'If the Sun and Moon should doubt,
They'd immediately go out.'

William Blake, from 'Auguries of Innocence'

The Falcon Carol

The falcon flew from dark to dark
Drew silver from the Northern Star
And headed for the crinkled hills,
The rivers, lakes and waterfalls
    To find the source of light on earth
    The source of light on earth.

And as three weary pilgrim kings
Looked up and saw his glittering wings
The falcon saw a darkened town
A stable glowing like a crown
    And knew that he had found the truth
    That he had found the truth.

The falcon hovered like a star
His wings spun out a spirit fire
That drew the kings inside the shed:
The child asleep in his straw bed
    Was dreaming of a silver bird
    Was dreaming of a bird.

His task now done, the falcon rose
A spark ablaze with joyful news;
He lit the stars, he lit the moon
Then vanished in the arc of sun
That dawned beyond the Southern Cross
    Beyond the Southern Cross.

The Shadow

Would lope behind him up the mountains
Whistling a tune or resting, hands on hips,
And stroll with him through fields of waist-high wheat
Listening to his distracted murmurings;
It sat beside him on the rain-drenched boat
That reared up, whale-like, on the lake, and sang
A song of comfort only he could hear;
He could not see it in the starlit garden
But it was kneeling there, with palms raised up.
When he was executed on the hill
It merged into the shadow of the tree
The stormlight cast across the face of earth,
Waiting until the spirit left his body;
And in the silence of the place of tombs
When he shone like a thousand burning candles
It had already gone back home
To join the dark beyond the light, to wait
For him, its earthly shadow, to return.

Groenendaal

He sits against a trunk and bends
His knees, a lectern for his book;
Thoughts fly and land like birds around
The glade, unless he makes them still,
When, as they say, a glow appears
Above his head and he reaches for
The spirit tree that's upside down
Its branches fanned towards the earth
Its roots in heaven, so he climbs
Till he can see – above the woods
Of Soignes – the very ends of earth,
Snail weavings of rivers, puddle lakes,
Cities like little castles; and below
A speck of life, a man – himself
His face upturned towards his gaze,
Both paralysed between two worlds
Each one unsure of where he is
Or where he wants to be just then
And waiting for the other to return.

Angels and Harvesters

As thoughts arrive
From god knows where,
Or sun breaks through
A fraying cloud
Emboldening a patch
Of trees, or grass,
They just appeared
From nowhere
Among the harvesters
The field a world
Of cutting, gathering,
Cutting, gathering.
Their outlines sometimes
Flickering brighter,
They walked between
The bending figures
Curious
Pausing to watch,
Like ancestors
Almost remembering
The world they'd left,
Or foreigners
Amused to see
The same things done.
They moved around
Unseen by all —
Unless one glimpsed,
Perhaps, light thicken,

A glassy movement,
As air can wobble
On summer days.
And then they went
Walked into nothing
Just left the world
Without ceremony
Unless it was
The swish of scythes
The swish of scythes

Origen

The slow awakening of summer
Courtyards of Alexandria again
Adrip with bundled honeysuckle
A wine cup warming in the sun
Such sweetness from the Song of Songs!
Let him kiss me with the kisses
Of his mouth.
      Unbearable
The season and the rising flood
Of love, unbearable the stench
Of ripeness in the groins, a ripeness
That pushes him, a harvesting –
And relief, one sickle-moon slash
Two tiny worlds cupped in his hand.

Deserted

'Prayer means shedding of thoughts.'
– EVAGRIUS PONTICUS

My heaven is a stripping of the mind.
I make this glittering desert be a desert
The burning rock, rock, blue sky just sky
Until they are pristine; but then I find

The desert leads me to its opposite
Noise-vomiting Constantinople,
And sky reminds me of the boundless sea
Of Marmara, the reek of fish and salt.

And rock? Her skin on which I freely roved
That sent me as an exile to this place
Of desert, sky and rock, a paradise
Until a daydream of her gasping love

Propels me from my cave, my cell,
Into a glittering burning blue-skied hell.

The Pram Pusher's Tale

I stop and let a car career and swerve,
Continue bobbling the pram down the road
Anticipating bends, switching sides
To escape a sudden silent vehicle
Until relief! I turn off down a lane
Which opens up with trees on either flank;
A spine of grass, weeds, moss divides
The crumbly putty-coloured surface,
With its shadow play of shifting leaves.
Banks melt and spray their beggars' arms
Of briars, dusty blackberries.
I pause before the effort of the climb.

Looking down, I watch her watching eyes,
Bemused and focusing, the tiny lashes flickering.
Amazed by light and god knows what,
She is speechless, receiving messages –
Her eyes are ears, listening
To outer space or some forgotten land
Puzzled, as if a déjà vu were fading like a dream;
And in her eyes I can almost see the trees
Above, their veterans' medals struck by sun
Their branches tasselling gaps of light.

Stationary but moving
There's nothing she can do but look,
Receive the light and wonder at the wonder,
The fluent universe of colours;
For everything flows

In shapes and textures, shades and brilliance
Which have no names, significance.

★

In her I see myself as I am not –
Wonderless, searching more haphazardly
For meaning the more the years slip by
Half fearing some diabolic paradox
That the truth I hope to find
Cannot be found by searching
But only stumbled on by accident
Or granted freely, if at all,
But that I cannot know this
Until I have searched until dementia.
My will impels me, impelled in turn
By a memory of timelessness
A blessèd opening to another world,
A moment many years ago
Which left me helpless as a baby.

Incapacitated, confined to bed
I felt the past squirm up beneath me
A litany of unoriginal sins
More damaged pride than anything
But crippling in intensity.
Then after time, in meditation, prayer
Accompanied by gentle breathing
A crisis of remembering would pass
And there might come a sense of peace
The rip-cord of a parachute released
Silkily, floating through my being.

Each day the pattern would repeat itself:
The breathing loosening the body
An ebb and flow, ebb and flow
That led to subtle shifts of lightness;
Then stronger moments of expansion
Would lift and soften consciousness,
Erase incoming scatterings of thought
And bring about a silence,
A sphere without a boundary
Without a centre.
The sense of being sharpened, purified,
Of sympathy awakening
In measure with the fading of the self.

Day after day the peace intensified
Until one morning
My body started losing its solidity
My mind its thought – as usual,
The peacefulness pulsed in
With sudden starts like electric shocks
But too serene, soft-edged to be a shock
And still the peace kept coming on,
Implosions of graduated lightness
Deepening the space of the interior
Pushing its outer edge beyond control
And nothing could be done,
My disappearing self
Could only marvel at the process;
Then it happened –
The splintering of mental membrane
And flesh dissolving – a flash
A wave, atomic blinding
The ingress of obliteration

No inside or outside
A drowning in radiance
As if a holy presence had descended
And found an emptiness it had to flood,
There was no me, no thought, no body
Just new-born helplessness;
And simultaneously my heart released
A joy that blossomed uncontrollably
So physical, tingling, undirected,
Circulating in veins of light
As if the sun, risen in my core,
Had unified creation
And I was that creation.

And then it ended.

The self I thought had disappeared returned.
Although there'd been no thought, no body,
My mindlessness it seems still harboured
A minuscule materializing fear –
Despite the overflowing joy –
The fear that if I had no me
I would disintegrate, go mad, or die,
So something stirred, and forced me back to earth.

A reservoir of peacefulness remained
For days, for weeks, leaking drip by drip
A living presence which became a memory
Receding like the letters on a gravestone
A hungry ghost demanding to be fed
The light again, just as it was,
Complaining at the lack of silence
The tumbling in of hopes and fears

Dismays and pleasures, listlessness,
On which it fed like blood.

★

Decades have passed. I have another self
A pramful of anxieties
A source of love as well –
She is amazed by everything
Which passes overhead:
The flotsam of the moulting trees
Serrated silhouettes of crows
A sky without horizons.
Pusher and pushed, slow-moving comet,
She the cone and I the tail,
Snailing around this undulating circuit
All circumference and no centre
We pass familiar constellations:
The village pub and post office, the old grey church,
The yard with the dilapidated van
The road with overhanging trees
The glebe lands and the graveyard –
I've come to know exactly when
To cross the road or dodge a rut or pot-hole
To tip the pram to counteract the camber.
Each daily round's a layer of my life
Peeled off, irrevocably lost,
I leave the house and come back just the same
Indifferent to the fields and trees and sky
Insensible to anything but random thoughts
But haunted by light, and by her face
Deep limestone eyes
Searching into space like mine
Almost remembering paradise.

Jacob Boehme's Revelation

I wonder what he said that night
To his wife, the butcher's daughter,
The girl from Görlitz, earthy stock,
Who knew the inside of a carcass
As if it were a sewing box.
I see them lying there in bed
In self-inflicted silence
Their two worlds back to back
And he beside himself to tell her
The miracle he'd had that day
How, in a shock –
Like Peter when he realised
His preacher friend was the messiah –
The world had changed,
As if the wind had dropped,
The sun had burnt the seal of cloud
And with great strokes of warmth
Was slowing down the world
And he had seen beneath the surfaces
Of things, the movement of pure life
But how could he describe it?
The stems of grasses, weeds –
A thousand flametips of green –
Sap treacling through the trees
The air refined and dizzy
With tingling minute stars
Like clouds of silver gnats.

And now he's lying on his back
His eyes bright, remembering;

His lips tight around the words
Already dying in his throat
And he waiting not for revelations
Or another vision, but for a snore
A thud, a lolling arm across his chest,
A leg of lamb, drained of blood.

Visiting Julian of Norwich

We left the glare, the creaking laughter
Of rooks outside the church; stepped in.
No movement, noise, disturbed the dust
Within the banners of light the sun
Shone through the lancets onto stone.

We always felt a presence there,
As if there were an unseen cat
Haloed in a ginger pool of warmth,
Or friendly ghost kneeling at the back.

We found ourselves tip-toeing
Towards her cell, its aperture
An open gate between two worlds.
A cough, a whisper of her name
Seemed a shouted imposition;
Her slow approaching silhouetted hood
Looked like the angel of death's.

She listened to our loose confessions
And tales of lust and petty thieveries
And violence at the hands of others
And let silence be the judge.

It was the words she never said,
The looks we never saw
That clambered through us
As we retreated, met the sudden day
And quickly slipped our penitence,

Relieved to see the sharp horizon,
The spire, the mill, the five-roads' cross,
While she dissolved again to shadow
And a world without circumference.

The Song of Richard Rolle

In thinning winter cloud the sun
Finds petals of a Yorkshire rose;
The chapel light softens the stone
Around his knees and calloused toes

And he is deep in holy fire –
Although his nose and fingers freeze
His heart's a furnace and transforms
His godly thoughts to melodies

Of such a sweetness he's impelled
To sing full-chested, eyes shut tight,
Propelling songs to paradise –
Cascades of them – so loud they might

Drown out the angels, wake the saints
As on the last day; yet these psalms
Which shake the galleries of heaven
Lie silent in his prayer-pressed palms.

Sinner

i.m. Marguerite Porete, died in Paris, 1 June, 1310

Without a will no one can sin, she said.
Who cannot sin except the Lord?
We didn't want her dead

But she insisted on spreading lies
To simpletons and miscreants;
We had to stop her heresies.

Besides, she was a *pseudo-mulier*
Not fish or fowl, but smelling of them both
In the smoke that purified the square

Her face a wilting fleur-de-lys
Above the sackcloth of her body.
She had some dignity

Until the flames' red claws
Were gripping at her face
And carried out god's law –

Screeching like a thousand geese
The crowd let out a choral groan
When gold broke from her eyes.

But we were sanguine: the pyre
Released the soul she wanted god to enter
And sent it weeping to eternal fire.

That night we dumped her ashes in the Seine –
'Let her preach to fishes
About the will and its annihilation!'

Without a will no one can sin.
We did not sin: our will was god's.
Our work was holy doctrine

Our reasoning was unassailably strong,
We had a thousand years of learning.
Why did she swear that we were wrong?

Unless her words were not her own –
Then whose? Who spoke that filth?
Who gave her that conviction

If not the devil? No one spouts
With that intensity unless mad, evil;
Or touched by god, which she was not.

We had to safeguard others from her yeast,
Her hatred for us. She had to die.
She had to die – so help me Christ.

Tauler

Domini canis, he dared
To sniff out the poor,
Administered; the bedside air

Of pestilence hissed
From each half-cautious door
Like malicious gossip.

No use his shining pulpit verses
To swollen heads with turnip tongues.
Yet just his coming, his cloaked darkness

Brought light
And gave the almost dead new lungs
And eyes of evening swallows, alert

Above the tipped horizon
Of fields of swaying radiance.

Tobacco, Psalms and Bloodletting

I sometimes think back to my youth
Remembering the heavy sack of sin on my shoulders
And I bent double so it seemed
Across the fields, with scarecrows hung on crosses,
Along straight roads that led to nowhere,
Weighed down in ditches, barns, the hollow trees
    I slept in;
And how I searched like a pig for acorns
For someone to administer the truth,
To take the sack away;
I tried two men of god:
The first one said *tobacco, that's your man,*
It will not rid you of your weight
But it is good for easing pain;
And you should also sing the psalms,
They will distract you from your ruminations;
How can you sing of Zion and think of sin?
The second holy man suggested *bloodletting,*
It rids the body of its pompous need for god's salvation.
That's what I thought about within
The forest of my transformation,
Spiders threading their rigging across wet blades of grass,
    tobacco;
The wren up-tailed and blown about, *psalms*;
King-cups and wild garlic by the marshy stream,
    bloodletting;

And then that queer old morning
There came the stripes of sun through trees,
Illuminating things by chance it seemed at first.

I stared at leaves, tufts of grass now tipped with fire,
And everything appeared to be connected,
The little bits of world ran into one another
And I was part of that confluence
Standing like an angel on a chequerboard of light
And in a trance or slowing down of time
I moved into another world
My heart unclenching, like a fist becoming hand;
It came to me that nothing need be pressed by sin
In the full opening of the heart,
And with that realisation
Something like forgiveness poured in, or out,
My shoulders cast their burden off
My back at last began to straighten
And in a state of weightlessness I rose
High above the fields and villages of Leicestershire
High above the curious streets of Lichfield
High above the spires of London
And never really came back.

Hildegard and Volmar

We would be sitting in her room
Talking about an illness of the soul
Or inessentials of the day, or listening
To noises in the yard below
Then suddenly a puzzlement
Would creep up on her eyes
Tighten her lips into a patient smile
Or look of mildest irritation
As if she could not quite remember
Some herb, or novice.
I'd test her with a whispered question
And when she did not answer
I knew: her eyes would open deeper,
So blue and with a strange liquidity
As if the Rhine was flowing into them,
Her cheeks relaxing – and her mouth;
Her breathing rhythmic as a cat's,
Exhaling such a peacefulness
I'd hardly want to stir
But stilled my hands and feet
Embarrassed by my grossness
During these times of delicacy;
Within the walls of quietude
My senses opened up or deepened:
The melancholy call of crows
A breeze escaping round the chapel
Steps fading on the flagstones
A boatman's solitary shout.
We sat alone in different worlds,
I'd watch the sun reduce

The shadow on the ledge
Or wonder where she was,
Perhaps revisiting that valley
So green in its particulars
The air was like the dust of emeralds.
I often questioned why the lord
Selected her not me.
Was it the purity of thought or heart?

And yet I was contented
With what this world provided me,
The river sweeping light downstream
The fragrance of ale, the touch
Of parchment, good ink and pen.
It might be minutes or an hour
Before the lustre left her eyes;
Her fingers were the first to move,
Then blinking, a deflating sigh,
Her look of momentary sadness,
A frown as now, returned to earth,
She attempted to forgive
My pouched world-weary eyes
As I attempted to forgive
Her journey to the indescribable
Which my obedient hand
Was scribbling down.

Dark Night of the Soul

What are the use of senses
That only magnify
The details of a cell
A cesspit in Toledo
Where jailers have the masks of monks
And beat with famished rage?
A blacker line
Frames the bolted door,
The touch of waste and stone,
Stench of straw, taste
Of sweat, dry body salt,
The sound of steps that mark
Patterns of persecution

Day after day
Or is it
Night after night?

Sometimes, without the stars,
The sun-dial's blade of shadow,
Time flies off from its rhythm
A sort of death, no less,
And in the emptiness
The desolation of nothing
The blindness of a box of night
My soul surges, escapes
The prison in the prison
Soars up and over new worlds
An eagle

Afloat on the breath of life
Like god above creation –

My loved one is the mountains
And lonely wooded valleys
Strange islands
Rushing streams
Whispering sensual winds.

Winter Tree

i.m. Nicolas Herman (Brother Lawrence), d. 1691

The forest of Lorraine had died
Of cold; the air, too gripped for snow,
Had frozen tracks of boots to fossils.
He stood there all alone inside
The limbo of eighteen years of life,
Hung between a squandered past
And dread of future days, unfit
For soldiery, books, a wife.
He stared across the field: the tree
Was silhouetted like a gallows,
Its upraised fingers begging god
To start the world again, to free
The warmth. Then as the first snow fell
A realisation thawed his blood –
Though stripped and scourged to death the tree
Was holding tight in every cell
The forms of blossoms, fruits and leaves
All waiting to unfurl their colours
In depths of green. He smiled as if
He were the sun, in such relief
That against the shrivellings of reason
Life can never be extinguished;
Bled cold and starved of light it waits,
And waits, for the right unrolling season.

By James Harpur from Anvil

The Dark Age

'*The Dark Age* is a supremely beautiful collection... It challenges us to have knowledge, to be readers, to be un-modern.'

THOMAS McCARTHY, *Southword*

'His poetry, always strongly imbued with a sense of the sacred, makes great play of light's spiritual resonance... his brilliant imagery and luxuriant natural descriptions offer plenty to enjoy.'

SARAH CROWN, *The Guardian*

Oracle Bones

'James Harpur is not in the least like anyone else... His is an amazingly consistent voice, compelling in its intensity. If you're brave enough, read him. He will take you into a world you will find difficult to forget.'

R. J. BAILEY, *Envoi*

'The volume of poetry published this year [2001] that I have returned to most often...'

ANTHONY HAYNES, *The Tablet* (Books of the Year)

The Monk's Dream

'James Harpur's second book is disciplined, intelligent and repays several readings... *The Monk's Dream* is an intricate exploration of death – not death alone, but the mystery that surrounds the experience... In all, *The Monk's Dream* is a finely weighted and balanced work of elegy.'

RICHARD TYRELL, *Times Literary Supplement*

A Vision of Comets

'James Harpur's first collection [has] a sense of the sacred running in parallel to the quotidian, and while the poems often reach into the exotic or esoteric, they are nevertheless accurately and cleanly made observances of a world the senses have access to.'

MARY RYAN, *Poetry Ireland Review*